Wage Labour and Capital

KARL MARX

Table of Contents

Wage Labour and Capital..1

    KARL MARX...1

    INTRODUCTION..1

WAGE LABOUR AND CAPITAL..9

    I...9

    II...13

    III...19

    IV...23

    V..28

Wage Labour and Capital

KARL MARX

Kessinger Publishing reprints thousands of hard–to–find books!

Visit us at http://www.kessinger.net

- INTRODUCTION
- WAGE LABOUR AND CAPITAL

    - I
    - II
    - III
    - IV
    - V

PUBLISHER'S NOTE

The present edition of Karl Marx's *Wage Labour and Capital*,[1] including the Introduction by Frederick Engels,[2] follows the German edition of 1891. The translation is based on previous ones, while some changes have been made for conformity with the German original.

INTRODUCTION

The following work appeared as a series of leading articles in the *Neue Rheinische Zeitung* from April 4, 1849 onwards. It is based on the lectures delivered by Marx in 1847 at the German Workers' Society in Brussels.[3] The work as printed remained a fragment; the words at the end of No. 269: "To be continued," remained unfulfilled in consequence of the events which just then came crowding one after another: the invasion of Hungary by the Russians, the insurrections in Dresden, Iserlohn, Elberfeld, the Palatinate and Baden,[4] which led to the suppression of the newspaper itself (May 19, 1849). The manuscript of the continuation was not found among Marx's papers after his death.

Wage Labour and Capital has appeared in a number of editions as a separate publication in pamphlet form, the last being in 1884, by the Swiss Co-operative Press, Hottingen-Zurich. The editions hitherto published retained the exact wording of the original. The present new edition, however, is to be circulated in not less than 10,000 copies as a propaganda pamphlet, and so the question could not but force itself upon me whether under these circumstances Marx himself would have approved of an unaltered reproduction of the original.

In the forties, Marx had not yet finished his critique of political economy. This took place only towards the end of the fifties. Consequently, his works which appeared before the first part of *A Contribution to the Critique of Political Economy* (1859) differ in some points from those written after 1859, and contain expressions and whole sentences which, from the point of view of the later works, appear askew and even incorrect. Now, it is self-evident that in ordinary editions intended for the general public this earlier point of view also has its place, as a part of the intellectual development of the author, and that both author and public have an indisputable right to the unaltered reproduction of these older works. And I should not have dreamed of altering a word of them.

It is another thing when the new edition is intended practically exclusively for propaganda among workers. In such a case Marx would certainly have brought the old presentation dating from 1849 into harmony with his new point of view. And I feel certain of acting as he would have done in undertaking *for this edition* the few alterations and additions which are required in order to attain this object in all essential points. I therefore tell the reader beforehand: this is not the pamphlet as Marx wrote it in 1849 but approximately as he would have written it in 1891. The actual text, moreover is circulated in so many copies that this will suffice until I am able to reprint it again, unaltered, in a later complete edition.

My alterations all turn on one point. According to the original, the worker sells his *labour* to the capitalist for wages; according to the present text he sells his labour *power*. And for this alteration I owe an explanation. I owe it to the workers in order that they may see it is not a case here of mere juggling with words, but rather of one of the most important points in the whole of political economy. I owe it to the bourgeois, so that they can convince themselves how vastly superior the uneducated workers, for whom one can easily make comprehensible the most difficult economic analyses, are to our supercilious "educated people" to whom such intricate questions remain insoluble their whole life long.

Classical political economy took over from industrial practice the current conception of the manufacturer, that he buys and pays for the *labour* of his workers. This conception had been quite adequate for the business needs, the book–keeping and price calculations of the manufacturer. But, naively transferred to political economy, it produced there really wondrous errors and confusions.

Economics observes the fact that the prices of all commodities, among them also the price of the commodity that it calls "labour," are continually changing; that they rise and fall as the result of the most varied circumstances, which often bear no relation whatever to the production of the commodities themselves, so that prices seem, as a rule, to be determined by pure chance. As soon, then, as political economy made its appearance as a science, one of its first tasks was to seek the law which was concealed behind this chance apparently governing the prices of commodities, and which, in reality, governed this very chance. Within the prices of commodities, continually fluctuating and oscillating, now upwards and now downwards, political economy sought for the firm central point around which these fluctuations and oscillations turned. In a word, it started from the *prices* of commodities in order to look for the *value* of the commodities as the law controlling prices, the value by which all fluctuations in price are to be explained and to which finally they are all to be ascribed. Classical economics then found that the value of a commodity is determined by the labour contained in it, requisite for its production. With this explanation it contented itself. And we also can pause here for the time being. I will only remind the reader, in order to avoid misunderstandings, that this explanation has nowadays become totally inadequate. Marx was the first thoroughly to investigate the value–creating quality of labour and he discovered in so doing that not all labour apparently, or even really, necessary for the production of a commodity adds to it under all circumstances a magnitude of value which corresponds to the quantity of labour expended. If therefore today we say offhandedly with economists like Ricardo that the value of a commodity is determined by the labour necessary for its production, we always in so doing imply the reservations made by Marx. This suffices here; more is to be found in Marx's *A Contribution to the Critique of Political Economy*, 1859, and the first volume of *Capital*. [5]

But as soon as the economists applied this determination of value by labour to the commodity "labour," they fell into one contradiction after another. How is the value of "labour" determined? By the necessary labour contained in it. But how much labour is contained in the labour of a worker for a day, a week, a month, a year? The labour of a day, a week, a month, a year. If labour is the measure of all values, then indeed we can express the "value of labour" only in labour. But we know absolutely nothing about the value of an hour of labour, if we only know that it is equal to an hour of labour. This brings us not a hair's breadth nearer the goal; we keep on moving in a circle.

Classical economics, therefore, tried another tack. It said: The value of a commodity is equal to its cost of production. But what is the cost of production of labour? In order to answer this question, the economists have to tamper a little with logic. Instead of investigating the cost of production of labour itself, which unfortunately cannot be ascertained, they proceed to investigate the cost of production of the *worker*. And this can be ascertained. It varies with time and circumstance, but for a given state of society, a given locality and a given branch of production, it too is given, at least within fairly narrow limits. We live today under the domination of capitalist production, in which a large, ever-increasing class of the population can live only if it works for the owners of the means of production — the tools, machines, raw materials and means of subsistence — in return for wages. On the basis of this mode of production, the cost of production of the worker consists of that quantity of the means of subsistence — or their price in money — which, on the average, is necessary to make him capable of working, keep him capable of working, and to replace him, after his departure by reason of old age, sickness or death, with a new worker — that is to say, to propagate the working class in the necessary numbers. Let us assume that the money price of these means of subsistence averages three marks a day.

Our worker, therefore, receives a wage of three marks a day from the capitalist who employs him. For this, the capitalist makes him work, say, twelve hours a day, calculating roughly as follows:

Let us assume that our worker — a machinist — has to make a part of a machine which he can complete in one day. The raw material — iron and brass in the necessary previously prepared form — costs twenty marks. The consumption of coal by the steam engine, and the wear and tear of this same engine, of the lathe and the other tools which our worker uses represent for one day, and reckoned by his share of their use, a value of one mark. The wage for one day, according to our assumption, is three marks. This makes twenty–four marks in all for our machine part. But the capitalist calculates that he will obtain, on an average, twenty–seven marks from his customers in return, or three marks more than his outlay.

Whence come the three marks pocketed by the capitalist? According to the assertion of classical economics, commodities are, on the average, sold at their values, that is, at prices corresponding to the amount of necessary labour contained in them. The average price of our machine part — twenty–seven marks — would thus be equal to its value, that is, equal to the labour embodied in it. But of these twenty–seven marks, twenty–one marks were values already present before our machinist began work. Twenty marks were contained in the raw materials, one mark in the coal consumed during the work, or in the machines and tools which were used in the process and which were diminished in their efficiency by the value of this sum. There remain six marks which have been added to the value of the raw material. But according to the assumption of our economists themselves, these six marks can only arise from the labour added to the raw material by our worker. His twelve hours' labour has thus created a new value of six marks. The value of his twelve hours' labour would, therefore, be equal to six marks. And thus we would at last have discovered what the "value of labour" is.

"Hold on there!" cries our machinist. "Six marks? But I have received only three marks! My capitalist swears by all that is holy that the value of my twelve hours' labour is only three marks, and if I demand six he laughs at me. How do you make that out?"

If previously we got into a vicious circle with our value of labour, we are now properly caught in an insoluble contradiction. We looked for the value of labour and we have found more than we can use. For the worker, the value of the twelve hours' labour is three marks, for the capitalist it is six marks, of which he pays three to the worker as wages and pockets three for himself. Thus labour would have not one but two values and very different values into the bargain!

The contradiction becomes still more absurd as soon as we reduce to labour time the values expressed in money. During the twelve hours' labour a new value of six marks is created. Hence, in six hours three marks — the sum which the worker receives for twelve hours' labour. For twelve hours' labour the worker receives as an equivalent value the product of six hours' labour. Either, therefore, labour has two values, of which one is double the size of the other, or twelve equals six! In both cases we get pure nonsense.

Turn and twist as we will, we cannot get out of this contradiction, as long as we speak of the purchase and sale of labour and of the value of labour. And this also happened to the economists. The last offshoot of classical economics, the Ricardian school, was wrecked mainly by the insolubility of this contradiction. Classical economics had got into a blind alley. The man who found the way out of this blind alley was Karl Marx.

What the economists had regarded as the cost of production of "labour" was the cost of production not of labour but of the living worker himself. And what this worker sold to the capitalist was not his labour. "As soon as his labour actually begins," says Marx, "it has already ceased to belong to him; it can therefore no longer be sold by him."[6] At the most, he might sell his future labour, that is, undertake to perform a certain amount of work in a definite time. In so doing, however, he does not sell labour (which would first have to be performed) but puts his labour power at the disposal of the capitalist for a definite time (in the case of time work) or for the purpose of a definite output (in the case of piece–work) in return for a definite payment: he hires out, or sells, his labour power. But this labour power has grown together with his person and is inseparable from it. Its cost of production, therefore, coincides with his cost of production; what the economists called the cost of production of labour is really the cost of production of the worker and consequently of his labour power. And so we can go back from the cost of production of labour power to the value of labour power and determine the amount of socially necessary labour requisite for the production of labour power of a particular quality, as Marx has done in the chapter on the buying and selling of labour power. (Kapital, Band IV, 3. [7])

Now what happens after the worker has sold his labour power to the capitalist, that is, placed it at the disposal of the latter in return for a wage — day wage or piece wage — agreed upon beforehand? The capitalist takes the worker into his workshop or factory, where all the things necessary for work — raw materials, auxiliary materials (coal, dyes, etc.), tools, machines — are already to be found. Here the worker begins to drudge. His daily wage may be, as above, three marks — and in this connection it does not make any difference whether he earns it as day wage or piece wage. Here also we again assume that in twelve hours the worker by his labour adds a new value of six marks to the raw materials used up, which new value the capitalist realizes on the sale of the finished piece of work. Out of this he pays the worker his three marks; the other three marks he keeps for himself. If, now, the worker creates a value of six marks in twelve hours, then in six hours he creates a value of three marks. He has, therefore, already repaid the capitalist the counter–value of the three marks contained in his wages when he has worked six hours for him. After six hours' labour they are both quits, neither owes the other a pfennig.

"Hold on there!" the capitalist now cries. "I have hired the worker for a whole day, for twelve hours. Six hours, however, are only half a day. So go right on working until the other six hours are up — only then shall we be quits!" And, in fact, the worker has to comply with his contract "voluntarily" entered into, according to which he has pledged himself to work twelve whole hours for a labour product which costs six hours of labour.

It is just the same with piece wages. Let us assume that our worker makes twelve items of a commodity in twelve hours. Each of these costs two marks in raw materials and depreciation and is sold at two and a half marks. Then the capitalist, on the same assumptions as before, will give the worker twenty–five pfennigs per item; that makes three marks for twelve items, to earn which the worker needs twelve hours. The capitalist receives thirty marks for the twelve items; deduct twenty–four marks for raw materials and de preciation and there remain six marks, of which he pays three marks to the worker in wages and pockets three marks. It is just as above. Here, too, the worker works six hours for himself, that is, for replacement of his wages (half an hour in each of the twelve hours), and six hours for the capitalist.

The difficulty over which the best economists came to grief, so long as they started out from the value of "labour," vanishes as soon as we start out from the value of "labour *power* " instead. In our present–day capitalist society, labour power is a commodity, a commodity like any other, and yet quite a peculiar commodity. It has, namely, the peculiar property of being a value–creating power, a source of value, and, indeed, with suitable treatment, a source of more value than it itself possesses. With the present state of production, human labour power not only produces in one day a greater value than it itself possesses and costs; with every new scientific discovery, with every new technical invention, this surplus of its daily product over its daily cost increases, and therefore that portion of the labour day in which the worker works to produce the replacement of his day's wage decreases; consequently, on the other hand, that portion of the labour day in which he has to *make a present* of his labour to the capitalist without being paid for it increases.

Wage Labour and Capital

And this is the economic constitution of the whole of our present–day society: it is the working class alone which produces all values. For value is only another expression for labour, that expression whereby in our present–day capitalist society is designated the amount of socially necessary labour contained in a particular commodity. These values produced by the workers do not, however, belong to the workers. They belong to the owners of the raw materials, machines, tools and the funds for advances which allow these owners to buy the labour power of the working class. From the whole mass of products produced by it, the working class, therefore, receives back only a part for itself. And as we have just seen, the other part, which the capitalist class keeps for itself and at most has to divide with the class of landowners, becomes larger with every new discovery and invention, while the part falling to the share of the working class (reckoned per head) either increases only very slowly and inconsiderably or not at all, and under certain circumstances may even fall.

But these discoveries and inventions which supersede each other at an ever–increasing rate, this productivity of human labour which rises day by day to an extent previously un heard of, finally gives rise to a conflict in which the present–day capitalist economy must perish. On the one hand, immeasurable riches and a superfluity of products which the purchasers cannot cope with; on the other hand, the great mass of society proletarianized, turned into wage–workers, and precisely for that reason made incapable of appropriating for themselves this superfluity of products. The division of society into a small, excessively rich class and a large, propertyless class of wage–workers results in a society suffocating from its own superfluity, while the great majority of its members is scarcely, or even not at all, protected from extreme want. This state of affairs becomes daily more absurd and — more unnecessary. It *must* be abolished, it *can* be abolished. A new social order is possible in which the present class differences will have disappeared and in which — perhaps after a short transitional period involving some privation, but at any rate of great value morally — through the planned utilization and extension of the already existing enormous productive forces of all members of society, and with uniform obligation to work, the means for existence, for enjoying life, for the development and employment of all bodily and mental faculties, will be available in an equal measure and in ever–increasing fullness. And that the workers are becoming more and more determined to win this new social order will be demonstrated on both sides of the ocean by May the First, tomorrow, and by Sunday, May 3.[8]

Frederick Engels

London, April 30, 1891

WAGE LABOUR AND CAPITAL

I

From various quarters we have been reproached with not having presented the *economic relations* which constitute the material foundation of the present class struggles and national struggles. We have designedly touched upon these relations only where they directly forced themselves to the front in political conflicts.

The point was, above all, to trace the class struggle in current history, and to prove empirically by means of the historical material already at hand and which is being newly created daily, that, with the subjugation of the working class which had created the events of February and March,[9] its opponents were simultaneously defeated — the bourgeois republicans in France and the bourgeois and peasant classes which were fighting feudal absolutism throughout the continent of Europe; that the victory of the "honest republic" in France was at the same time the downfall of the nations that had responded to the February Revolution by heroic wars of independence; finally, that Europe, with the defeat of the revolutionary workers, had relapsed into its old double slavery, the *Anglo–Russian* slavery. The June struggle in Paris, the fall of Vienna, the tragicomedy of Berlin's November 1848, the desperate exertions of Holand, Italy and Hungary, the starving of Ireland into submission — these were the chief factors which characterized the European class struggle between bourgeoisie and working class and by means of which we proved that every revolutionary upheaval, however remote from the class struggle its goal may appear to be, must fail until the revolutionary working class is victorious, that every social reform remains a utopia until the proletarian revolution and the feudalistic counter–revolution cross swords in a *world war*. In our presentation, as in reality,

9

Wage Labour and Capital

Belgium and *Switzerland* were tragicomic genre–pictures akin to caricature in the great historical *tableau*, the one being the model state of the bourgeois monarchy, the other the model state of the bourgeois republic, both of them states which imagine themselves to be as independent of the class struggle as of the European revolution.

Now, after our readers have seen the class struggle develop in colossal political forms in 1848, the time has come to deal more closely with the economic relations themselves on which the existence of the bourgeoisie and its class rule, as well as the slavery of the workers, are founded.

We shall present in three large sections: 1) the relation of *wage labour to capital*, the slavery of the worker, the domination of the capitalist; 2) *the inevitable destruction of the middle bourgeois classes and of the so–called burgher estate under the present system* ; 3) *the commercial subjugation and exploitation of the bourgeois classes of the various European nations* by the despot of the world market — *England*.

We shall try to make our presentation as simple and popular as possible and shall not presuppose even the most elementary notions of political economy. We wish to be understood by the workers. Moreover, the most remarkable ignorance and confusion of ideas prevails in Germany in regard to the simplest economic relations, from the accredited defenders of the existing state of things down to the *socialist miracle workers* and the *unrecognized political geniuses* in which fragmented Germany is even richer than in sovereign princes.

Now, therefore, for the first question: *What are wages? How are they determined?*

If workers were asked: "What are your wages?" one would reply: "I get a mark a day from my boss"; another, "I get two marks," and so on. According to the different trades to which they belong, they would mention different sums of money which they receive from their respective bosses for the performance of a particular piece of work, for example, weaving a yard of linen or typesetting a printed sheet. In spite of the variety of their statements, they would all agree on one point: wages are the sum of money paid by the capitalist for a particular labour time or for a particular output of labour.

The capitalist, it seems, therefore, *buys* their labour with money. They *sell* him their labour for money. But this is merely the appearance. In reality what they sell to the capitalist for money is their labour *power*. The capitalist buys this labour power for a day, a week, a month, etc. And after he has bought it, he uses it by having the workers work for the stipulated time. For the same sum with which the capitalist has bought their labour power, for example, two marks, he could have bought two pounds of sugar or a definite amount of any other commodity. The two marks, with which he bought two pounds of sugar, are the *price* of the two pounds of sugar. The two marks, with which he bought twelve hours' use of labour power, are the price of twelve hours' labour. Labour power, therefore, is a commodity, neither more nor less than sugar. The former is measured by the clock, the latter by the scales.

The workers exchange their commodity, labour power, for the commodity of the capitalist, for money, and this exchange takes place in a definite ratio. So much money for so long a use of labour power. For twelve hours' weaving, two marks. And do not the two marks represent all the other commodities which I can buy for two marks? In fact, therefore, the worker has exchanged his commodity, labour power, for other commodities of all kinds and that in a definite ratio. By giving him two marks, the capitalist has given him so much meat, so much clothing, so much fuel, light, etc., in exchange for his day's labour. Accordingly, the two marks express the ratio in which labour power is exchanged for other commodities, the *exchange value* of his labour power. The exchange value of a commodity, reckoned in *money*, is what is called its *price*. *Wages* are only a special name for the price of labour power, commonly called the *price of labour*, for the price of this peculiar commodity which has no other repository than human flesh and blood.

Let us take any worker, say, a weaver. The capitalist supplies him with the loom and yarn. The weaver sets to work and the yarn is converted into linen. The capitalist takes possession of the linen and sells it, say, for twenty marks. Now are the wages of the weaver a *share* in the linen, in the twenty marks, in the product of his labour? By no means. Long before the linen is sold, perhaps long before its weaving is finished, the weaver has received his wages. The capitalist, therefore, does not pay these wages with the money which he will obtain from the linen, but with money already in reserve. Just as the loom and the yarn are not the product of the weaver to whom they are supplied by his employer, so likewise with the commodities which the weaver receives in exchange for his commodity, labour power. It was possible that his employer found no purchaser at all for his linen. It was possible that he did not get even the amount of the wages by its sale. It is possible that he sells it very profitably in comparison with the weaver's wages. All that has nothing to do with the weaver. The capitalist buys the labour power of the weaver with a part of his available wealth, of his capital, just as he has bought the raw material — the yarn — and the instrument of labour — the loom — with another part of his wealth. After he has made these purchases, and these purchases include the labour power necessary for the production of linen, he produces only with the *raw materials and instruments of labour belonging to him.* For the latter include now, true enough, our good weaver as well, who has as little share in the product or the price of the product as the loom has.

Wages are, therefore, not the worker's share in the commodity produced by him. Wages are the part of already existing commodities with which the capitalist buys a definite amount of productive labour power as such.

Labour power is, therefore, a commodity which its possessor, the wage-worker, sells to capital. Why does he sell it? In order to live.

But the exercise of labour power, labour, is the worker's own life-activity, the manifestation of his own life. And this *life-activity* he sells to another person in order to secure the necessary *means of subsistence.* Thus his life-activity is for him only a means to enable him to exist. He works in order to live. He does not even reckon labour as part of his life, it is rather a sacrifice of his life. It is a commodity which he has made over to another. Hence, also, the product of his activity is not the object of his activity. What he produces for himself is not the silk that he weaves, not the gold that he draws from the mine, not the palace that he builds. What he produces for himself is *wages*, and silk, gold, palace resolve themselves for him into a definite quantity of the means of subsistence, perhaps into a cotton jacket, some copper coins and a lodging in a cellar. And the worker, who for twelve hours weaves, spins, drills, turns, builds, shovels, breaks stones, carries loads, etc. — does he hold this twelve hours' weaving, spinning, drilling, turning, building, shovelling, stone-breaking to be a manifestation of his life, to be life? On the contrary, life begins for him where this activity ceases, at table, in the tavern, in bed. The twelve hours' labour, on the other hand, has no meaning for him as weaving, spinning, drilling, etc., but as *earnings*, which bring him to the table, to the tavern, into bed. If the silkworm were to spin in order to continue its existence as a caterpillar, it would be a complete wage-worker. Labour power was not always a *commodity*. Labour was not always wage labour, that is, *free labour*. The *slave* did not sell his labour power to the slave owner, any more than the ox sells its services to the peasant. The slave, together with his labour power, is sold once and for all to his owner. He is a commodity which can pass from the hand of one owner to that of another. He is *himself* a commodity, but the labour power is not *his* commodity. The *serf* sells only a part of his labour power. He does not receive a wage from the owner of the land; rather the owner of the land receives a tribute from him.

The serf belongs to the land and renders to the owner of the land the fruits thereof. The *free labourer*, on the other hand, sells himself and, indeed, sells himself piecemeal. He auctions off eight, ten, twelve, fifteen hours of his life, day after day, to the highest bidder, to the owner of the raw materials, instruments of labour and means of subsistence, that is, to the capitalist. The worker belongs neither to an owner nor to the land, but eight, ten, twelve, fifteen hours of his daily life belong to him who buys them. The worker leaves the capitalist to whom he hires himself whenever he likes, and the capitalist discharges him whenever he thinks fit, as soon as he no longer gets any profit out of him, or not the anticipated profit. But the worker, whose sole source of livelihood is the sale of his labour power, cannot leave the *whole class of purchasers, that is , the capitalist class,* without renouncing his existence. He belongs not to this or that capitalist but to the *capitalist class* , and, moreover, it is his business to dispose of himself, that is, to find a purchaser within this capitalist class.

Now, before going more closely into the relation between capital and wage labour, we shall present briefly the most general relations which come into consideration in the determination of wages.

Wages, as we have seen, are the *price* of a definite commodity, of labour power. Wages are, therefore, determined by the same laws that determine the price of every other commodity. The question, therefore, is, *how is the price of a commodity determined?*

II

By what is the *price* of a commodity determined?

By the competition between buyers and sellers, by the relation of demand to supply, of want to offer. Competition, by which the price of a commodity is determined, is *three—sided.*

The same commodity is offered by various sellers. With goods of the same quality, the one who sells most cheaply is certain of driving the others out of the field and securing the greatest sale for himself. Thus, the sellers mutually contend among themselves for sales, for the market. Each of them desires to sell, to sell as much as possible and, if possible, to sell alone, to the exclusion of the other sellers. Hence, one sells cheaper than another. Consequently, *competition* takes place *among the sellers*, which *depresses* the price of the *commodities* offered by them.

But *competition* also takes place *among the buyers*, which in its turn *causes* the commodities offered to *rise* in price.

Finally, *competition* occurs *between buyers and sellers* ; the former desire to buy as cheaply as possible, the latter to sell as dearly as possible. The result of this competition between buyers and sellers will depend upon how the two above—mentioned sides of the competition are related, that is, whether the competition is stronger in the army of buyers or in the army of sellers. Industry leads two armies into the field against each other, each of which again carries on a battle within its own ranks, among its own troops. The army whose troops beat each other up the least gains the victory over the opposing host.

Let us suppose there are 100 bales of cotton on the market and at the same time buyers for 1,000 bales of cotton. In this case, therefore, the demand is ten times as great as the supply. Competition will be very strong among the buyers, each of whom desires to get one, and if possible all, of the hundred bales for himself. This example is no arbitrary assumption. We have experienced periods of cotton crop failure in the history of the trade when a few capitalists in alliance have tried to buy, not one hundred bales, but all the cotton stocks of the world. Hence, in the example mentioned, one buyer will seek to drive the other from the held by offering a relatively higher price per bale of cotton. The cotton sellers, who see that the troops of the enemy army are engaged in the most violent struggle among themselves and that the sale of all their hundred bales is absolutely certain, will take good care not to fall out among themselves and depress the price of cotton at the moment when their adversaries are competing with one another to force it up. Thus, peace suddenly descends on the army of the sellers. They stand facing the buyers as *one* man, fold their arms philosophically, and there would be no bounds to their demands were it not that the offers of even the most persistent and eager buyers have very definite limits.

If, therefore, the supply of a commodity is lower than the demand for it, then only slight competition, or none at all, takes place among the sellers. In the same proportion as this competition decreases, competition increases among the buyers. The result is a more or less considerable rise in commodity prices.

It is well known that the reverse case with a reverse result occurs more frequently. Considerable surplus of supply over demand; desperate competition among the sellers; lack of buyers; disposal of goods at ridiculously low prices.

But what is the meaning of a rise, a fall in prices; what is the meaning of high price, low price? A grain of sand is high when examined through a microscope, and a tower is low when compared with a mountain. And if price is determined by the relation between supply and demand, what determines the relation between supply and demand?

Let us turn to the first bourgeois we meet. He will not reflect for an instant but, like another Alexander the Great, will cut this metaphysical knot with the multiplication table. If the production of the goods which I sell has cost me 100 marks, he will tell us, and if I get 110 marks from the sale of these goods, within the year of course — then that is sound, honest, legitimate profit. But if I get in exchange 120 or 130 marks, that is a high profit; and if I get as much as 200 marks, that would be an extraordinary, an enormous profit. What, therefore, serves the bourgeois as his *measure* of profit? The *cost of production* of his commodity. If he receives in exchange for this commodity an amount of other commodities which it has cost less to produce, he has lost. If he receives in exchange for his commodity an amount of other commodities the production of which has cost more, he has gained. And he calculates the rise or fall of the profit according to the degree in which the exchange value of his commodity stands above or below zero — the *cost of production*.

We have thus seen how the changing relation of supply and demand causes now a rise and now a fall of prices, now high, now low prices. If the price of a commodity rises considerably because of inadequate supply or disproportionate increase of the demand, the price of some other commodity must necessarily have fallen proportionately, for the price of a commodity only expresses in money the ratio in which other commodities are given in exchange for it. If, for example, the price of a yard of silk material rises from five marks to six marks, the price of silver in relation to silk material has fallen and likewise the prices of all other commodities that have remained at their old prices have fallen in relation to the silk. One has to give a larger amount of them in exchange to get the same amount of silks. What will be the consequence of the rising price of a commodity? A mass of capital will be thrown into that flourishing branch of industry and this influx of capital into the domain of the favoured industry will continue until it yields the ordinary profits or, rather, until the price of its products, through over–production, sinks below the cost of production.

Conversely, if the price of a commodity falls below its cost of production, capital will be withdrawn from the production of this commodity. Except in the case of a branch of industry which has become obsolete and must, therefore, perish, the production of such a commodity, that is, its supply, will go on decreasing owing to this flight of capital until it corresponds to the demand, and consequently its price is again on a level with its cost of production or, rather, until the supply has sunk below the demand, that is, until its price rises again above its cost of production, *for the current price of a commodity is always either above or below its cost of production.*

We see how capital continually migrates in and out, out of the domain of one industry into that of another. High prices bring too great an immigration and low prices too great an emigration.

We could show from another point of view how not only supply but also demand is determined by the cost of production. But this would take us too far away from our subject.

We have just seen how the fluctuations of supply and demand continually bring the price of a commodity back to the cost of production. *The real price of a commodity, it is true, is always above or below its cost of production ; but rise and fall reciprocally balance each other,* so that within a certain period of time, taking the ebb and flow of the industry together, commodities are exchanged for one another in accordance with their cost of production, their price, therefore, being determined by their cost of production.

This determination of price by cost of production is not to be understood in the sense of the economists. The economists say that the *average price* of commodities is equal to the cost of production; that this is a *law*. The anarchical movement, in which rise is compensated by fall and fall by rise, is regarded by them as chance. With just as much right one could regard the fluctuations as the law and the determination by the cost of production as chance, as has actually been done by other economists. But it is solely these fluctuations, which, looked at more closely, bring with them the most fearful devastations and, like earthquakes, cause bourgeois society to tremble to its foundations — it is solely in the course of these fluctuations that prices are determined by the cost of production. The total movement of this disorder is its order. In the course of this industrial anarchy, in this movement in a circle competition compensates, so to speak, for one excess by means of another.

We see, therefore, that the price of a commodity is determined by its cost of production in such manner that the periods in which the price of this commodity rises above its cost of production are compensated by the periods in which it sinks below the cost of production, and vice versa. This does not hold good, of course, for separate, particular industrial products but only for the whole branch of industry. Consequently, it also does not hold good for the individual industrialist but only for the whole class of industrialists.

The determination of price by the cost of production is equivalent to the determination of price by the labour time necessary for the manufacture of a commodity, for the cost of production consists of 1) raw materials and depreciation of instruments, that is, of industrial products the production of which has cost a certain amount of labour days and which, therefore, represent a certain amount of labour time, and 2) direct labour, the measure of which is, precisely, time.

Now, the same general laws that regulate the price of commodities in general of course also regulate *wages*, the *price of labour.*

Wages will rise and fall according to the relation of supply and demand, according to the turn taken by the competition between the buyers of labour power, the capitalists, and the sellers of labour power, the workers. The fluctuations in wages correspond in general to the fluctuations in prices of commodities. *Within these fluctuations , however, the price of labour will be determined by the cost of production, by the labour time necessary to produce this commodity — labour power.*

What, then, is the cost of production of labour power?

Wage Labour and Capital

It is the cost required for maintaining the worker as a worker and of developing him into a worker.

The less the period of training, therefore, that any work requires, the smaller is the cost of production of the worker and the lower is the price of his labour, his wages. In those branches of industry in which hardly any period of apprenticeship is required and where the mere bodily existence of the worker suffices, the cost necessary for his production is almost confined to the commodities necessary for keeping him alive and capable of working. The *price of his labour* will, therefore, be determined by the *price of the neccssary means of subsistence.*

Another consideration, however, also comes in. The manufacturer in calculating his cost of production and, accordingly, the price of the products takes into account the wear and tear of the instruments of labour. If, for example, a machine costs him 1,000 marks and wears out in ten years, he adds 100 marks annually to the price of the commodities so as to be able to replace the worn-out machine by a new one at the end of ten years. In the same way, in calculating the cost of production of simple labour power, there must be included the cost of reproduction, whereby the race of workers is enabled to multiply and to replace worn-out workers by new ones. Thus the depreciation of the worker is taken into account in the same way as the depreciation of the machine.

The cost of production of simple labour power, therefore, amounts to the *cost of existence and reproduction of the worker.* The price of this cost of existence and reproduction constitutes wages. Wages so determined are called the *wage minimum.* This wage minimum, like the determination of the price of commodities by the cost of production in general, does not hold good for the *single individual* but for the *species.* Individual workers, millions of workers, do not get enough to be able to exist and reproduce themselves; *but the wages of the whole working class* level down, within their fluctuations, to this minimum.

Now that we have arrived at an understanding of the most general laws which regulate wages like the price of any other commodity, we can go into our subject more specifically.

III

Capital consists of raw materials, instruments of labour and means of subsistence of all kinds, which are utilized in order to produce new raw materials, new instruments of labour and new means of subsistence. All these component parts of capital are creations of labour, products of labour, *accumulated labour*. Accumulated labour which serves as a means of new production is capital.

So say the economists.

What is a Negro slave? A man of the black race. The one explanation is as good as the other.

A Negro is a Negro. He only becomes a slave in certain relations. A cotton–spinning jenny is a machine for spinning cotton. It becomes *capital* only in certain relations. Torn from these relationships it is no more capital than gold in itself is *money* or sugar the price of sugar.

In production, men not only act on nature but also on one another. They produce only by co–operating in a certain way and mutually exchanging their activities. In order to produce, they enter into definite connections and relations with one another and only within these social connections and relations does their action on nature, does production, take place.

These social relations into which the producers enter with one another, the conditions under which they exchange their activities and participate in the whole act of production, will naturally vary according to the character of the means of production. With the invention of a new instrument of warfare, firearms, the whole internal organization of the army necessarily changed; the relationships within which individuals can constitute an army and act as an army were transformed and the relations of different armies to one another also changed.

Thus the social relations within which individuals produce, *the social relations of production, change, are transformed, with the change and development of the material means of production, the productive forces. The relations of production in their totality constitute what are called the social relations, society, and, specifically, a society at a definite stage of historical development*, a society with a peculiar, distinctive character. *Ancient* society, *feudal* society, *bourgeois* society are such totalities of production relations, each of which at the same time denotes a special stage of development in the history of mankind.

Capital, also, is a social relation of production. *It is a bourgeois production relation*, a production relation of bourgeois society. Are not the means of subsistence, the instruments of labour, the raw materials of which capital consists, produced and accumulated under given social conditions, in definite social relations? Are they not utilized for new production under given social conditions, in definite social relations? And is it not just this definite social character which turns the products serving for new production into *capital*?

Capital consists not only of means of subsistence, instruments of labour and raw materials, not only of material products; it consists just as much of *exchange values*. All the products of which it consists are *commodities*. Capital is, therefore, not only a sum of material products; it is a sum of commodities, of exchange values, of *social magnitudes*.

Capital remains the same, whether we put cotton in place of wool, rice in place of wheat or steamships in place of railways, provided only that the cotton, the rice, the steamships — the body of capital — have the same exchange value, the same price as the wool, the wheat, the railways in which it was previously incorporated. The body of capital can change continually without the capital suffering the slightest alteration.

But while all capital is a sum of commodities, that is, of exchange values, not every sum of commodities, of exchange values, is capital.

Every sum of exchange values is an exchange value. Every separate exchange value is a sum of exchange values. For instance, a house that is worth 1,000 marks is an exchange value of 1,000 marks. A piece of paper worth a pfennig is a sum of exchange values of one–hundred hundredths of a pfennig. Products which are exchangeable for others are *commodities*. The particular ratio in which they are exchangeable constitutes their *exchange value* or, expressed in money, their *price*. The quantity of these products can change nothing in their quality of being *commodities* or representing an *exchange value* or having a definite *price*. Whether a tree is large or small it is a tree. Whether we exchange iron for other products in ounces or in hundredweights, does this make any difference in its character as commodity, as exchange value? It is a commodity of greater or lesser value, of higher or lower price, depending upon the quantity.

How, then, does any amount of commodities, of exchange values, become capital?

By maintaining and multiplying itself as an independent social *power*, that is, as the power *of a portion of society*, by means of its *exchange for direct, living labour power*. The existence of a class which possesses nothing but its capacity to labour is a necessary prerequisite of capital.

It is only the domination of accumulated, past, materialized labour over direct, living labour that turns accumulated labour into capital.

Capital does not consist in accumulated labour serving living labour as a means for new production. It consists in living labour serving accumulated labour as a means for maintaining and multiplying the exchange value of the latter.

What takes place in the exchange between capitalist and wage–worker?

The worker receives means of subsistence in exchange for his labour power, but the capitalist receives in exchange for his means of subsistence labour, the productive activity of the worker, the creative power whereby the worker not only replaces what he consumes but *gives to the accumulated labour a greater value than it previously possessed*. The worker receives a part of the available means of subsistence from the capitalist. For what purpose do these means of subsistence serve him? For immediate consumption. As soon, however, as I consume the means of subsistence, they are irretrievably lost to me unless I use the time during which I am kept alive by them in order to produce new means of subsistence, in order during consumption to create by my labour new values in place of the values which perish in being consumed. But it is just this noble reproductive power that the worker surrenders to the capitalist in exchange for means of subsistence received. He has, therefore, lost it for himself.

Let us take an example: a tenant farmer gives his day labourer five silver groschen a day. For these five silver groschen the labourer works all day on the farmer's field and thus secures him a return of ten silver groschen. The farmer not only gets the value replaced that he has to give the day labourer; he doubles it. He has therefore employed, consumed, the five silver groschen that he gave to the labourer in a fruitful, productive manner. He has bought with the five silver groschen just that labour and power of the labourer which produces agricultural products of double value and makes ten silver groschen out of five. The day labourer, on the other hand, receives in place of his productive power, the effect of which he has bargained away to the farmer, five silver groschen, which he exchanges for means of subsistence, and these he consumes with greater or lesser rapidity. The five silver groschen have, therefore, been consumed in a double way, *reproductively* for capital, for they have been exchanged for labour power[*] which produced ten silver groschen, *unproductively* for the worker, for they have been exchanged for means of subsistence which have disappeared forever and the value of which he can only recover by repeating the same exchange with the farmer. *Thus capital presupposes wage labour ; wage labour presupposes capital. They reciprocally condition the existence of each others they reciprocally bring forth each other.*

Does a worker in a cotton factory produce merely cotton textiles? No, he produces capital. He produces values which serve afresh to command his labour and by means of it to create new values.

Capital can only increase by exchanging itself for labour power, by calling wage labour to life. The labour power of the wage–worker can only be exchanged for capital by increas ing capital, by strengthening the power whose slave it is. *Hence, increase of capital is increase of the proletariat, that is, of the working class.*

The interests of the capitalist and those of the worker are, therefore, *one and the same*, assert the bourgeois and their economists. Indeed! The worker perishes if capital does not employ him. Capital perishes if it does not exploit labour power, and in order to exploit it, it must buy it. The faster capital intended for production, productive capital, increases, the more, therefore, industry prospers, the more the bourgeoisie enriches itself and the better business is, the more workers

---

* The term "labour power" was not added here by Engels but had already been in the text Marx published in the *Neue Rheinische Zeitung. — Ed.* does the capitalist need, the more dearly does the worker sell himself.

Wage Labour and Capital

The indispensable condition for a tolerable situation of the worker *is, therefore, the fastest possible growth of productive capital.*

But what is the growth of productive capital? Growth of the power of accumulated labour over living labour. Growth of the domination of the bourgeoisie over the working class. If wage labour produces the wealth of others that rules over it, the power that is hostile to it, capital, then the means of employment, that is, the means of subsistence, flow back to it from this hostile power, on condition that it makes itself afresh into a part of capital, into the lever which hurls capital anew into an accelerated movement of growth.

To say that the interests of capital and those of the workers are one and the same is only to say that capital and wage labour are two sides of one and the same relation. The one conditions the other , just as usurer and squanderer condition each other.

As long as the wage–worker is a wage–worker his lot depends upon capital. That is the much–vaunted community of interests between worker and capitalist.

IV

If capital grows, the mass of wage labour grows, the number of wage-workers grows; in a word, the domination of capital extends over a greater number of individuals. Let us assume the most favourable case: when productive capital grows, the demand for labour grows; consequently, the price of labour, wages, goes up.

A house may be large or small; as long as the surrounding houses are equally small it satisfies all social demands for a dwelling. But let a palace arise beside the little house, and it shrinks from a little house to a hut. The little house shows now that its owner has only very slight or no demands to make; and however high it may shoot up in the course of civilization, if the neighbouring palace grows to an equal or even greater extent, the occupant of the relatively small house will feel more and more uncomfortable, dissatisfied and cramped within its four walls.

A noticeable increase in wages presupposes a rapid growth of productive capital. The rapid growth of productive capital brings about an equally rapid growth of wealth, luxury, social wants, social enjoyments. Thus, although the enjoyments of the worker have risen, the social satisfaction that they give has fallen in comparison with the increased enjoyments of the capitalist, which are inaccessible to the worker, in comparison with the state of development of society in general. Our desires and pleasures spring from society; we measure them, therefore, by society and not by the objects which serve for their satisfaction. Because they are of a social nature, they are of a relative nature.

In general, wages are determined not only by the amount of commodities for which I can exchange them. They embody various relations.

What the workers receive for their labour power is, in the first place, a definite sum of money. Are wages determined only by this money price?

In the sixteenth century, the gold and silver circulating in Europe increased as a result of the discovery of richer and more easily worked mines in America. Hence, the value of gold and silver fell in relation to other commodities. The workers received the same amount of coined silver for their labour power as before. The money price of their labour remained the same, and yet their wages had fallen, for in exchange for the same quantity of silver they received a smaller amount of other commodities. This was one of the circumstances which furthered the growth of capital and the rise of the bourgeoisie in the sixteenth century.

Let us take another case. In the winter of 1847, as a result of a crop failure, the most indispensable means of subsistence, cereals, meat, butter, cheese, etc., rose considerably in price. Assume that the workers received the same sum of money for their labour power as before. Had not their wages fallen? Of course. For the same money they received less bread, meat, etc., in exchange. Their wages had fallen, not because the value of silver had diminished, but because the value of the means of subsistence had increased.

Assume, finally, that the money price of labour remains the same while all agricultural and manufactured goods have fallen in price owing to the employment of new machinery, a favourable season, etc. For the same money the workers can now buy more commodities of all kinds. Their wages, therefore, have risen, just because the money value of their wages has not changed.

Wage Labour and Capital

Thus, the money price of labour, nominal wages, do not coincide with real wages, that is, with the sum of commodities which is actually given in exchange for the wages. If, therefore, we speak of a rise or fall of wages, we must keep in mind not only the money price of labour, the nominal wages.

But neither nominal wages, that is, the sum of money for which the worker sells himself to the capitalist, nor real wages, that is, the sum of commodities which he can buy for this money, exhaust the relations contained in wages.

Wages are, above all, also determined by their relation to the gain, to the profit of the capitalist — comparative, relative wages.

Real wages express the price of labour in relation to the price of other commodities; relative wages, on the other hand, express the share of direct labour in the new value it has created in relation to the share which falls to accumulated labour, to capital.

We said above, page 19: "Wages are not the worker's share in the commodity produced by him. Wages are the part of already existing commodities with which the capitalist buys a definite amount of productive labour power as such." But the capitalist must replace these wages out of the price at which he sells the product produced by the worker; he must replace it in such a way that there remains to him, as a rule, a surplus over the cost of production expended by him, a profit. For the capitalist, the selling price of the commodity produced by the worker is divided into three parts: *first*, replacement of the price of the raw materials advanced by him together with replacement of the depreciation of the tools, machinery and other means of labour also advanced by him; *secondly*, the replacement of the wages advanced by him, and *thirdly*, the surplus left over, the capitalist's profit. While the first part only replaces *previously existing values*, it is clear that both the replacement of the wages and also the surplus profit of the capitalist are, on the whole, taken from the *new value created by the workers labour* and added to the raw materials. And *in this sense*, in order to compare them with one another, we can regard both wages and profit as shares in the product of the worker.

Real wages may remain the same, they may even rise, and yet relative wages may fall. Let us suppose, for example, that all means of subsistence have gone down in price by two thirds while wages per day have only fallen by one–third, that is to say, for example, from three marks to two marks. Although the worker can command a greater amount of commodities with these two marks than he previously could with three marks, yet his wages have gone down in relation to the profit of the capitalist. The profit of the capitalist (for example, the manufacturer) has increased by one mark; that is, for a smaller sum of exchange values which he pays to the worker, the latter must produce a greater amount of exchange values than before. The share of capital relative to the share of labour has risen. The division of social wealth between capital and labour has become still more unequal. With the same capital, the capitalist commands a greater quantity of labour. The power of the capitalist class over the working class has grown, the social position of the worker has deteriorated, has been depressed one step further below that of the capitalist.

What, then, *is the general law which determines the rise and fall of wages and profit in their reciprocal relation?*

They stand in inverse ratio to each other. Capital's share, *profit, rises in the same proportion as labour's share, wages, falls, and vice versa. Profit rises to the extent that wages fall* ; *it falls to the extent that wages rise.*

The objection will, perhaps, be made that the capitalist can profit by a favourable exchange of his products with other capitalists, by increase of the demand for his commodity, whether as a result of the opening of new markets, or as a result of a momentarily increased demand in the old markets, etc.; that the capitalist's profit can, therefore, increase by overreaching other capitalists, independently of the rise and fall of wages, of the exchange value of labour power; or that the capitalist's profit may also rise owing to the improvement of the instruments of labour, a new application of natural forces, etc.

First of all, it will have to be admitted that the result remains the same, although it is brought about in reverse fashion. True, the profit has not risen because wages have fallen, but wages have fallen because the profit has risen. With the same amount of other people's labour, the capitalist has acquired a greater amount of exchange values, without having paid more for the labour on that account; this means, therefore, that labour is paid less in proportion to the net profit which it yields the capitalist.

In addition, we recall that, in spite of the fluctuations in prices of commodities, the average price of every commodity, the ratio in which it is exchanged for other commodities, is determined by its *cost of production*. Hence the overreachings within the capitalist class necessarily balance one another. The improvement of machinery, new application of natural forces in the service of production, enable a larger amount of products to be created in a given period of time with the same amount of labour and capital, but not by any means a larger amount of exchange values. If, by the use of the spinning jenny, I can turn out twice as much yarn in an hour as before its invention, say, one hundred pounds instead of fifty, then in the long run I will receive for these hundred pounds no more commodities in exchange than formerly for the fifty pounds, because the cost of production has fallen by one–half, or because I can deliver double the product at the same cost.

Finally, in whatever proportion the capitalist class, the bourgeoisie, whether of one country or of the whole world market, shares the net profit of production within itself, the total amount of this net profit always consists only of the amount by which, on the whole, accumulated labour has been increased by direct labour. This total amount grows, therefore, in the proportion in which labour augments capital, that is, in the proportion in which profit rises in comparison with wages.

We see, therefore, that even if we remain *within the relation of capital and wage labour, the interests of capital and the interests of wage labour are diametrically opposed.*

A rapid increase of capital is equivalent to a rapid increase of profit. Profit can only increase rapidly if the price of labour, if relative wages, decrease just as rapidly. Relative wages can fall although real wages rise simultaneously with nominal wages, with the money value of labour, if they do not rise, however, in the same proportion as profit. If, for instance, in times when business is good, wages rise by five per cent, profit on the other hand by thirty per cent, then the comparative, the relative wages, have not *increased* but *decreased*.

Thus if the income of the worker increases with the rapid growth of capital, the social gulf that separates the worker from the capitalist increases at the same time, and the power of capital over labour, the dependence of labour on capital, likewise increases at the same time.

To say that the worker has an interest in the rapid growth of capital is only to say that the more rapidly the worker increases the wealth of others, the richer will be the crumbs that fall to him, the greater is the number of workers that can be employed and called into existence, the more can the mass of slaves dependent on capital be increased.

We have thus seen that:

Even the *most favourable situation* for the working class, the *most rapid possible growth of capital*, however much it may improve the material existence of the worker, does not remove the antagonism between his interests and the interests of the bourgeoisie, the interests of the capitalist. *Profit and wages* remain as before in *inverse proportion.*

If capital is growing rapidly, wages may rise; the profit of capital rises incomparably more rapidly. The material position of the worker has improved, but at the cost of his social position. The social gulf that divides him from the capitalist has widened.

Finally:

To say that the most favourable condition for wage labour is the most rapid possible growth of productive capital is only to say that the more rapidly the working class increases and enlarges the power that is hostile to it, the wealth that does not belong to it and that rules over it, the more favourable will be the conditions under which it is allowed to labour anew at increasing bourgeois wealth, at enlarging the power of capital, content with forging for itself the golden chains by which the bourgeoisie drags it in its train.

V

Are *growth of productive capital and rise of wages* really so inseparably connected as the bourgeois economists maintain? We must not take their word for it. We must not even believe them when they say that the fatter capital is, the better will its slave be fed. The bourgeoisie is too enlightened, it calculates too well, to share the prejudices of the feudal lord who makes a display by the brilliance of his retinue. The conditions of existence of the bourgeoisie compel it to calculate.

We must, therefore, examine more closely:

Wage Labour and Capital

How does the growth of productive capital affect wages?

If, on the whole, the productive capital of bourgeois society grows, a *more manifold* accumulation of labour takes place. The capitalists increase in number and extent. The *numerical increase* of the capitals increases the *competition between the capitalists.* The *increasing extent* of the capitals provides the means for *bringing more powerful labour armies with more gigantic instruments of war into the industrial battlefield.*

One capitalist can drive another from the field and capture his capital only by selling more cheaply. In order to be able to sell more cheaply without ruining himself, he must produce more cheaply, that is, raise the productive power of labour as much as possible. But the productive power of labour is raised, above all, by *a greater division of labour,* by a more universal introduction and continual improvement of *machinery.* The greater the labour army among whom labour is divided, the more gigantic the scale on which machinery is introduced, the more does the cost of production proportionately decrease, the more fruitful is labour. Hence, a general rivalry arises among the capitalists to increase the division of labour and machinery and to exploit them on the greatest possible scale.

If, now, by a greater division of labour, by the utilization of new machines and their improvement, by more profitable and extensive exploitation of natural forces, one capitalist has found the means of producing with the same amount of labour or of accumulated labour a greater amount of products, of commodities, than his competitors, if he can, for example, produce a whole yard of linen in the same labour time in which his competitors weave half a yard, how will this capitalist operate?

He could continue to sell half a yard of linen at the old market price; this would, however, be no means of driving his opponents from the field and of enlarging his own sales. But in the same measure in which his production has expanded, his need to sell has also increased. The more powerful and costly means of production that he has called into life *enable* him, indeed, to sell his commodities more cheaply, they *compel* him, however, at the same time *to sell more commodities,* to conquer a much *larger* market for his commodities; consequently, our capitalist will sell his half yard of linen more cheaply than his competitors.

The capitalist will not, however, sell a whole yard as cheaply as his competitors sell half a yard, although the production of the whole yard does not cost him more than the half yard costs the others. Otherwise he would not gain anything extra but only get back the cost of production by the exchange. His possibly greater income would be derived from the fact of having set a iarger capital into motion, but not from having made more of his capital than the others. Moreover, he attains the object he wishes to attain, if he puts the price of his goods only a small percentage lower than that of his competitors. He drives them from the field, he wrests from them at least a part of their sales, by *underselling* them. And, finally, it will be remembered that the current price always stands *above or below the cost of production*, according to whether the sale of the commodity occurs in a favourable or unfavourable industrial season. The percentage at which the capitalist who has employed new and more fruitful means of production sells above his real cost of production will vary, depending upon whether the market price of a yard of linen stands below or above its hitherto customary cost of production.

However, the *privileged position* of our capitalist is not of long duration; other competing capitalists introduce the same machines, the same division of labour, introduce them on the same or on a larger scale, and this introduction will become so general that the price of linen *is reduced* not only *below its old*, but *below its new cost of production.*

The capitalists find themselves, therefore, in the same position relative to one another as *before* the introduction of the new means of production, and if they are able to supply by these means double the product at the same price, they are now forced to supply the double product *below* the old price. On the basis of this new cost of production, the same game begins again. More division of labour, more machinery, enlarged scale of exploitation of machinery and division of labour. And again competition brings the same counteraction against this result.

We see how in this way the mode of production and the means of production are continually transformed, revolutionized, *how the division of labour is necessarily followed by greater division of labour , the application of machinery by still greater application of machinery, work on a large scale by work on a still larger scale.*

That is the law which again and again throws bourgeois production out of its old course and which compels capital to strain the productive forces of labour, *because it* has strained them, the law which gives capital no rest and continually whispers in its ear: Go

Wage Labour and Capital

on! Go on!

This law is none other than that which, within the fluctuations of trade periods, necessarily *levels out* the price of a commodity to its *cost of production.*

However powerful the means of production which a capitalist brings into the field, competition will make these means of production universal and from the moment when it has made them universal, the only result of the greater fruitfilness of his capital is that he must now supply *for the same price* ten, twenty, a hundred times as much as before. But, as he must sell perhaps a thousand times as much as before in order to outweigh the lower selling price by the greater amount of the product sold, because a more extensive sale is now necessary, not only in order to make more profit but in order to replace the cost of production — the instrument of production itself, as we have seen, becomes more and more expensive — and because this mass sale becomes a queston of life and death not only for him but also for his rivals, the old struggle begins again *all the more violently the more fruitful the already discovered means of production are. The division of labour and the application of machinery, therefore , will go on anew on an incomparably greater scale.*

Whatever the power of the means of production employed may be, competition seeks to rob capital of the golden fruits of this power by bringing the price of the commodicies back to the cost of production, by thus making cheaper producton — the supply of ever greater amounts of products for the same total price — an imperative law to the same extent as production can be cheapened, that is, as more can be produced with the same amount of labour. Thus the capitalist would have won nothing by his own exertions but the obligation to supply more in the same labour time, in a word, *more difficult conditions for the augmentation of the value of his capital.* While, therefore, competition continually pursues him with its law of the cost of production and every weapon that he forges against his rivals recoils against himself, the capitalist continually tries to get the better of competition by incessantly introducing new machines, more expensive, it is true, but producing more cheaply, and new division of labour in place of the old, and by not waiting until competition has rendered the new ones obsolete.

If now we picture to ourselves this feverish simultaneous agitation on the *whole world market*, it will be comprehensible how the growth, accumulation and concentration of capital results in an uninterrupted division of labour, and in the application of new and the perfecting of old machinery precipitately and on an ever more gigantic scale.

But how do these circumstances, which are inseparable from the growth of productive capital, affect the determination of wages?

The greater *division of labour* enables *one* worker to do the work of five, ten or twenty; it therefore multiplies com petition among the workers fivefold, tenfold and twentyfold The workers do not only compete by one selling himself cheaper than another; they compete by *one* doing the work of five, ten, twenty; and the *division of labour*, introduced by capital and continually increased, compels the workers to compete among themselves in this way.

Further, as the *division of labour* increases, labour *is simplified.* The special skill of the worker becomes worthless. He becomes transformed into a simple, monotonous productive force that does not have to bring intense bodily or intellectual faculties into play. His labour becomes a labour that anyone can perform. Hence, competitors crowd upon him on all sides, and besides we remind the reader that the more simple and easily learned the labour is, the lower the cost of production needed to master it, the lower do wages sink, for, like the price of every other commodity, they are determined by the cost of production.

Therefore, as labour becomes more unsatisfying, more repulsive, competition increases and wages decrease. The worker tries to keep up the amount of his wages by working more, whether by working longer hours or by producing more in one hour. Driven by want, therefore, he still further increases the evil effects of the division of labour. The result is that *the more he works the less wages he receives*, and for the simple reason that he competes to that extent with his fellow workers, hence makes them into so many competitors who offer themselves on just the same bad terms as he does himself, and that, therefore, in the last resort he *competes with himself, with himself as a member of the working class.*

Machinery brings about the same results on a much greater scale, by replacing skilled workers by unskilled, men by women, adults by children. It brings about the same results, where it is newly introduced, by throwing the hand workers onto the streets in masses, and, where it is developed, improved and replaced by more productive machinery, by discharging workers in smaller batches. We have portrayed above, in a hasty sketch, the industrial war of the capitalists among themselves; *this war has the peculiarity that its battles are won less by recruiting than by discharging the army of labour. The generals , the capitalists, compete with one another as to who can discharge most soldiers of industry.*

The economists tell us, it is true, that the workers rendered superfluous by machinery find new branches of employment.

They dare not assert directly that the same workers who are discharged find places in the new branches of labour The facts cry out too loudly against this lie. They really only assert that new means of employment will open up for *other component sections of the working class*, for instance, for the portion of the young generation of workers that was ready to enter the branch of industry which has gone under. That is, of course, a great consolation for the displaced workers. The capitalist gentlemen will never want for fresh exploitable flesh and blood, and will let the dead bury their dead. This is a consolation which the bourgeois give themselves rather than one which they give the workers. If the whole class of wage–workers were to be abolished owing to machinery, how dreadful that would be for capital which, without wage labour, ceases to be capital!

Let us suppose, however, that those directly driven out of their jobs by machinery, and the entire section of the new generation that was already on the watch for this employment, *find a new occupation*. Does any one imagine that it will be as highly paid as that which has been lost? *That would contradict all the laws of economics*. We have seen how modern industry always brings with it the substitution of a more simple, subordinate occupation for the more complex and higher one.

How, then, could a mass of workers who have been thrown out of one branch of industry owing to machinery find refuge in another, unless the latter *is lower, worse paid?*

The workers who work in the manufacture of machinery itself have been cited as an exception. As soon as more machinery is demanded and used in industry, it is said, there must necessarily be an increase of machines, consequently of the manufacture of machines, and consequently of the employment of workers in the manufacture of machines; and the workers engaged in this branch of industry are claimed to be skilled, even educated workers.

Wage Labour and Capital

Since the year 1840 this assertion, which even before was only half true, has lost all semblance of truth because ever more versatile machines have been employed in the manufacture of machinery, no more and no less than in the manufacture of cotton yarn, and the workers employed in the machinery factories, confronted by highly elaborate machines, can only play the part of highly unelaborate machines.

But in place of the man who has been discharged owing to the machine, the factory employs maybe *three* children and *one* woman! And did not the man's wages have to suffice for the three children and a woman? Did not the minimum of wages have to suffice to maintain and to propagate the race? What, then, does this favourite bourgeois phrase prove? Nothing more than that now four times as many workers' lives are used up in order to gain a livelihood for *one* worker's family.

Let us sum up: *The more productive capital grows, the more the division of labour and the application of machinery expands. The more the division of labour and the application of machinery expands , the more competition among the workers expands and the more their wages contract.*

In addition, the working class gains recruits from the *higher strata of society* also; a mass of petty industrialists and small rentiers are hurled down into its ranks and have nothing better to do than urgently stretch out their arms alongside those of the workers. Thus the forest of uplifted arms demanding work becomes ever thicker, while the arms themselves become ever thinner.

That the small industrialist cannot survive in a contest, one of the first conditions of which is to produce on an ever greater scale, that is, precisely to be a large and not a small industrialist, is self–evident.

That the interest on capital decreases in the same measure as the mass and number of capitals increase, as capital grows; that, therefore, the small rentier can no longer live on his interest but must throw himself into industry, and, consequently, help to swell the ranks of the small industrialists and thereby of candidates for the proletariat — all this surely requires no further explanation.

Finally, as the capitalists are compelled, by the movement described above, to exploit the already existing gigantic means of production on a larger scale and to set in motion all the mainsprings of credit to this end, there is a corresponding increase in industrial earthquakes, in which the trading world can only maintain itself by sacrificing a part of wealth, of products and even of productive forces to the gods of the nether world — in a word, *crises* increase. They become more frequent and more violent, if only because, as the mass of products, and consequently the need for extended markets, grows, the world market becomes more and more contracted fewer and fewer new markets remain available for exploitation, since every preceding crisis has subjected to world trade a market hitherto unconquered or only superficially exploited. But capital does not live only on labour. A lord, at once aristocratic and barbarous, it drags with it into the grave the corpses of its slaves, whole hecatombs of workers who perish in the crises. Thus we see: *if capital grows rapidly, competition among the workers grows incomparably more rapidly, that is, the means of employment, the means of subsistence, of the working class decrease proportionately so much the more, and, nevertheless, the rapid growth of capital is the most favourable condition for wage labour.*

----

[1] *Wage Labour and Capital* was written by Marx on the basis of a series of lectures he delivered at the German Workers' Society in Brussels in the second half of December 1847. A manuscript entitled "Wages," copied by Joseph Weydemeyer, has been preserved, which conforms almost entirely to the text published in the *Neue Rheinische Zeitung*. Early in 1848 Marx tried to publish the work in Brussels, but he had to give up the plan in consequence of his expulsion from Belgium.

The work was first published under the title of "Wage Labour and Capital' as a series of leading articles in the *Neue Rheinische Zeitung* of April 5–8 and 11, 1849. But the series was interrupted by Marx's temporary departure from Cologne and, subsequently, by the aggravation of the political situation in Germany and the termination of the publication of the paper.

Marx's articles carried in the *Neue Rheinische Zeitung* contributed to the dissemination of the ideas of scientific socialism among German workers. By the decision of the Committee of the Cologne Workers' Association, they were recommended for discussion in workers' associations in Cologne and other cities.

After the suppression of the *Neue Rheinische Zeitung*, Marx intended to publish *Wage Labour and Capital* in pamphlet form, but the plan did not materialize. The first separate edition of the work came out in Breslau in 1880 without Marx's participation, followed by a second edition published in the same city. With the participation of Engels, another edition was published in Hottingen–Zurich in 1884, which included a brief preface by Engels tracing the history of the work. A new edition for propaganda among workers, edited and prefaced by Engels, was published in 1891.

The text of *Wage Labour and Capital* remains incomplete. A draft outline of Marx's concluding lectures, which he worked out in December 1847 under the title of "Wages," complements the present work.   [Pub.Note]

Wage Labour and Capital

[2] The Introduction was written by Engels for a new edition of Karl Marx's *Wage Labour and Capital* published under his direction in Berlin in 1891. Engels began the Introduction by restating his preface to the 1884 edition of the same work. The pamphlet containing the Introduction was printed in large numbers of copies for the dissemination of Marx's economic teachings among the workers.

The Introduction appeared in workers' and socialist journals as a separate thesis and enjoyed a wide circulation. It was published, before the pamphlet came off the press, as a supplement to *Vorw* No. 109, May 13, 1891, under the title of "Wage Labour and Capital." A slightly abridged version was carried in the weekly Freiheit, No. 22, May 30, 1891; in the Italian journal Critica sociale, No. 10, July 10, 1891; in Le Socialiste, No. 44, July 22, 1891; in an almanac published by the French socialist magazine, Question sociale, in 1892, and in other publications.

The Introduction was included in all subsequent editions of Marx's work, which was translated into various languages on the basis of the 1891 edition. [Pub.Note]

[3] The German Workers' Society was founded by Marx and Engels in Brussels at the end of August 1847 for conducting political education and spreading the ideas of scientific communism among German workers residing in Belgium. Under the direction of Marx, Engels and their comrades–in–arms, the society became the legal rallying centre for revolutionary German proletarians in Belgium, and maintained direct contact with Flemish and Walloon workers' clubs. Later the best members of the society joined the Brussels section of the Communist League. The society ceased to function soon after the bourgeois February Revolution in France in 1848 as its members were arrested or banished by the Belgian police. [p.1]

[4] Reference is to the intervention carried out by tsarist troops in Hungary in 1849 for the purpose of suppressing the bourgeois revolution in the country and restoring the rule of the Austrian Hapsburg Dynasty there, and to the uprisings staged in Germany in support of the Imperial Constitution which was adopted by the Frankfort National Assembly on March 28, 1849 but rejected by the governments of most German states. The uprisings marked the final stage of the bourgeois democratic revolution in Germany. [p. 1]

[5] See Karl Marx, *A Contribution to the Critique of Political Economy* , International Publishers, New York, 1970, pp. 27–52; and Karl Marx, *Capital*, Charles H. Kerr and Company, Chicago, 1926, Vol. I, pp. 41–96. [p.4]

[6] See *Capital*, Chicago, 1926, Vol. I, p. 588. [p.8]

[7] *Ibid.*, pp. 185–96. [p.8]

[8] Engels refers here to the May Day celebrations in 1891. In some countries, such as Britain and Germany, May Day was celebrated on the first Sunday after May 1, which in 1891 fell on May 3. Mass rallies and demonstrations were held on May Day, 1891, by workers in many cities in Britain, Austria, Germany, France, Italy, Russia and other countries. [p.12]

Wage Labour and Capital

[9] This refers to the Revolution of February 23–24, 1848 in Paris, of March 13 in Vienna, and of March 18 in Berlin. [p. 15]

Printed in the United States
24871LVS00002B/41